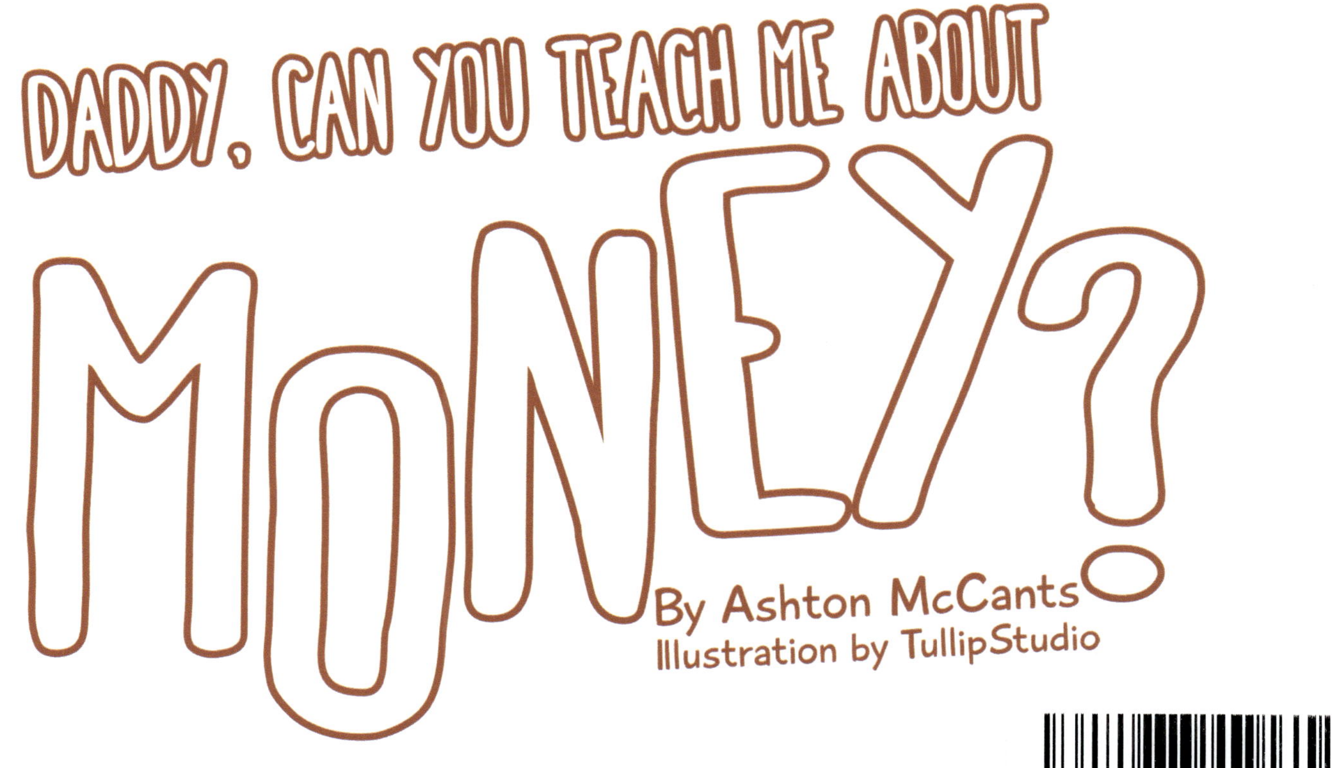
DADDY, CAN YOU TEACH ME ABOUT
MONEY?
By Ashton McCants
Illustration by TullipStudio

First Edition: March 2021

This book is dedicated to my son Tristan, for whom it was written and who inspired me to write it.

Tristan was getting older and was curious about everything. One Saturday, after he and his parents returned from the supermarket, he realized there was something that he needed to know. He saw an old dollar bill on the kitchen table and squinted at it.

“Daddy,” he said, “What is money and how does it work?”

“Good question,” Dad said. “Money is a form of currency exchanged for goods and services. It is used to pay for everything you see here – this home, food and your video games. We used money to pay for those things so that we can have them as our own.”

"Sounds easy," Tristan said.

"It's not that easy Tristan. Let's take a quick walk into town so that we can get a better idea of how money is used," Dad said.

"Okay Dad. Let me just grab some money from my piggy bank. I may see something that I want while we're there!" Tristan grabbed $1 and off they went. They went to the town square.

"Look around you Tristan. See how money is being used? Ms. Bailey is buying fish from the fish market, Mr. Robinson is paying the taxi man, Ms. Greene is walking out the supermarket with her groceries and even your friend Aiden headed home with a new pair of new shoes. Take a look at Mr. & Mrs. Ryan walking out of from Eazy Transactions. Do you know what they may have been doing in there?"

"Did they send money to someone?" Tristan asked.

Dad smiled, "That's a great guess! This is where some people in town go to pay their bills to keep their water and lights working for their home."

Tristan's head started to buzz. He'd begun to realize how important money was. He'd assumed that most of these things were free. He didn't realize that his video games, the Internet and the clothes he wore all cost money.

"Wow! It's like money is the sun and everything revolves around it." Tristan remembered a solar system project he did in school.

"That's a very cool way to put it son," his dad said.

As Tristan and his dad were talking, they overheard a conversation between Ms. Joy and the store clerk. "I'm sorry, Ms. Joy. It seems like you don't have enough money to pay for everything."

"I could have sworn I did..." Ms. Joy dug through her purse.

"Can't the store clerk just give her the rest of the money she needs for her things?" Tristan asked his dad.

"That's not necessarily how it works son," his dad explained.

"I wonder if I can help Ms. Joy." Tristan ran over to her.

"Excuse me Ms. Joy, I have $1 if you need it."

Ms. Joy's face exploded with a smile! "This is very sweet of you Tristan, but I think it's best you save your money so you can afford the things that you need. I can put a few items back so that I am able to afford my order. Just do me a favor... promise me that you will always save your money, okay?"
Tristan nodded."

"Oh! I almost forgot! Be sure to invest as well Tristan. Investing your money allows your money to grow without you needing to work for it. Investing your money is an awesome way to build wealth."

"Thank you Ms. Joy!" Tristan made note of those two things – saving and investing.

"That's great advice she gave you son. One day we will dive more into that, but let's talk about how money is earned."

Tristan immediately became distracted by this cool game in the video game store across the street. They had one of the newest games playing in the window on display.

Tristan noticed a sign that said, "$2 per 15 minutes play."

"Tristan?" His dad said.

"Yes dad?" He quickly looked up.

"You zoned out for a second there. What's got your attention?" His dad looked to see what caught his attention. "Oh! I see now. One of the games that you've been wanting is on display."

"Yea. Sorry about that Dad," Tristan said. "No need to be sorry Tristan. That is what it was designed to do," his Dad explained. "The store puts the game on display in the window to make you want to go in. If they can get you into the store, there is a good chance that you will spend money. This is called marketing," his dad said.

"Everything we buy has a cost. Money is normally earned through a job," his dad said.

"Mommy works from home. Is that a job?" Tristan asked.

"It is. Anything that you do to earn a salary or wage is a job."

Oh! I'm getting it now! You and mom take home all of the money that you earn and pay for things we need and some of the things we want right?" Tristan asked.

"Not all of it son," Dad answered.

"Do you give some of it to somebody?" Tristan asked, wondering whom it could be.

"Yes we do. We give some of it to the government in the form of taxes."

"The government?! Don't they have lots of money already? I saw a government person on TV yesterday with their very own driver! That must cost a lot of money. Why do they need your money dad?" Tristan stomped his feet a bit and crossed his arms.

Dad laughed, "Well, it helps the country provide for things that the people in it need, like the streets we drive on to take you to school. It is also used to build schools, hospitals and parks, along with other things. It is also used to pay teachers, our military and provide services like health care, public safety and education."

"Oh! That makes sense when you put it that way Dad," Tristan said.

"Taxes are very important son, even if we may not always like them or agree with where the money may be going," Dad explained.

"Thank you for the lesson Dad. This walk has really changed the way I look at money. I saw you and mom pay for things with money, but never knew how you earned it. Now I know that you and mommy have to work for it. You even have to give some of it away! I also know now that everything has a cost. I won't always have enough money to pay for the things that I want, but if I save my money, I can earn enough to be able to. Almost everything we do involves money." Tristan said as he looked at his money.

"We should try to do these money lessons more often since you're beginning to take an interest in your money and how it works. I see that you're still eyeing that game in the window. Did you want to go in and check it out?" His dad asked.

He really wanted to but now...

"No Dad. I'm ok. I can play the video games that I have at home. I'm going to save the money I have and maybe learn how to invest. Can you teach me more about how to do that?" Tristan said excitedly.

His dad chuckled, "I will son, but we should probably start heading home. It's almost dinner time."

"OK! I can't wait to tell Peyton and Jackson about what I learned today!" Tristan ran ahead.

Later that evening, he passed on his knowledge on to his younger siblings over dinner.

"I see you've inspired a future investor," Mom said to Dad.

Dad chuckled, "We have to teach them now so that they can make better choices than we did. The more they understand now, the better off they will be as they get older."

"I couldn't agree with you more," Mom said.

Tristan, Jackson and Peyton ran into the living room.

"Dad! Can you teach us about saving and investing?! Tristan was telling us all about your trip today!"

Dad smiled, "Sure guys. Have a seat. We have a lot to cover..."

Glossary

Currency – the type of money used in a particular place

Invest – to use money with the goal of making money

Job – work that you are paid to do

Marketing – activities that involve promoting or selling products

Money – an object exchanged for goods and services

Salary – a set amount of money paid to someone for a job.

Save – to put money away for use in the future

Taxes – money that a government requires people to pay

Bill – an amount owed for goods and services

Wage – an amount earned hourly for a job or service.

Wealth – having a lot of something valuable

www.ingramcontent.com/pod-product-compliance
Ingram Content Group UK Ltd.
Pitfield, Milton Keynes, MK11 3LW, UK
UKHW060115300726
14090UKWH00002B/207

* 9 7 9 8 7 3 1 8 7 0 9 4 8 *